D1542099

CHILLER MAZES

Vladimir Koziakin

SCHOLASTIC INC.
New York Toronto London Auckland Sydney

ISBN 0-590-33292-9

12 11 10 9   3 4 5/9

Printed in the U.S.A.   28

Are you ready for the challenge of *Chiller Mazes?*
All you need is a pencil — and for extra fun, a watch
to time yourself. Start at the arrow pointing in. With-
out crossing any lines, find your way along the *one*
path that leads to the arrow pointing out. You'll meet
a lot of your favorite fiends along the way, but don't
let them rattle you. You're the maze master!

Solutions appear in the back of the book.

Night Riders

Challenge Time: 2 minutes

They like to come out at night and drive you batty.

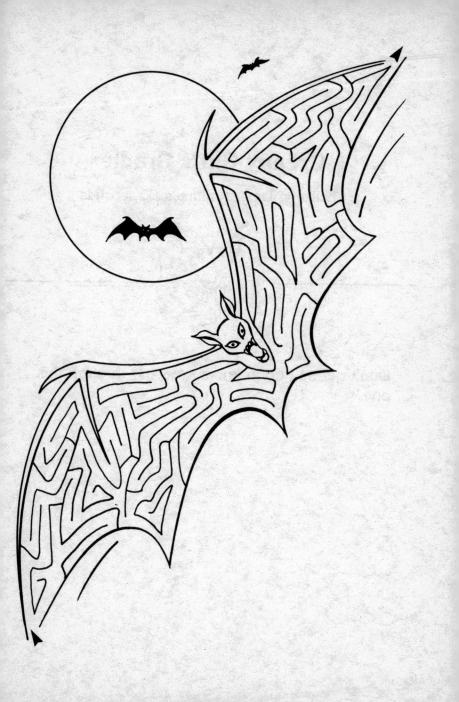

Creepy Cat's Cradle

Challenge Time: 3 minutes, 30 seconds

Don't get tied up in knots creeping through this one.

Vampire's Castle

Challenge Time: 4 minutes, 30 seconds

Do your good deed for the day — answer the call
for help from the vampire's castle.

Brain Drain

Challenge Time: 3 minutes, 30 seconds

This show-off will try to outsmart you, so keep your wits about you.

The Trembling Ghost

Challenge Time: 3 minutes, 30 seconds

Just remember — it's probably scared of you!

Venomous Vampire

Challenge Time: 1 minute, 30 seconds

Get away from those freaky fangs as fast as you can.

The Coffin Caper

You surely don't want to get lost inside this one.

The Witching Hour

Challenge Time: 5 minutes, 30 seconds

Midnight! It's no time to hang around here.

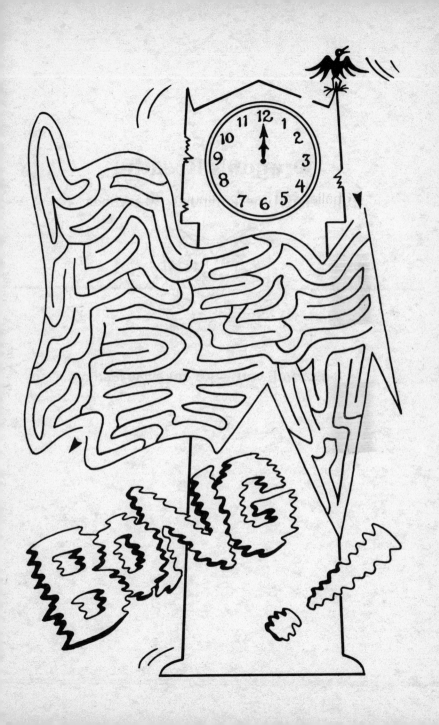

Dragon's Breath

Challenge Time: 2 minutes, 30 seconds

It'll scorch you — so get away fast!

Numb Skull

Challenge Time: 5 minutes

This one is a laugh a minute.

Witches Stew

Challenge Time: 4 minutes, 30 seconds

Don't take a second longer than the time limit or you'll go up in smoke.

Electronic Maniac

Challenge Time: 4 minutes

Pit your brains against the electrifying electronic maniac.

Unlucky Number?

Challenge Time: 5 minutes

Maybe number 13 will be lucky for you.

A Grave Situation

Challenge Time: 4 minutes, 45 seconds

Dig that crazy tombstone.

1801 - 2002

RIP

The Spider Trap

Challenge Time: 3 minutes, 15 seconds

It's guaranteed to tangle you up.

The Claw!

Challenge Time: 3 minutes, 15 seconds

It's got you coming and going!

Ghastly Ghoul

Challenge Time: 7 minutes

Keep your eye on the path and you'll zap this zany ghoul.

The Haunted House

Challenge Time: 6 minutes, 45 seconds

Enter at your own risk!

Weirdwolf

Challenge Time: 5 minutes, 30 seconds

Is it a weirdwolf or a werewolf — or both?

U.F.O. Oh, Oh!

Challenge Time: 6 minutes

If you're not through in 6 minutes, *you'll* be an unidentified flying object!

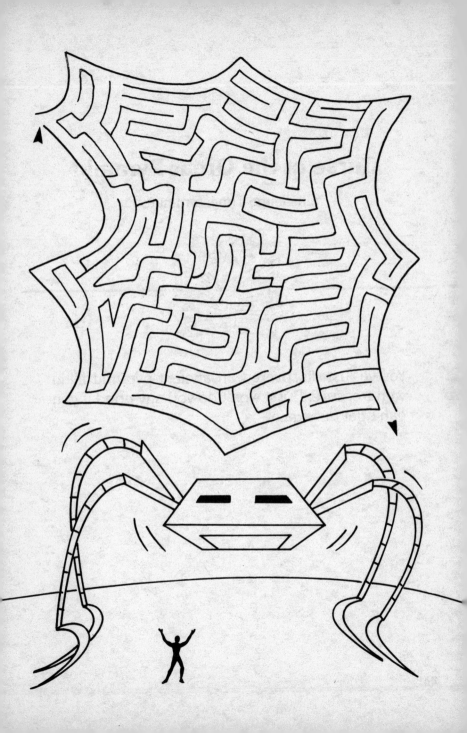

Curse of the Great Pyramid

Challenge Time: 6 minutes

You've just discovered an ancient pyramid filled with treasure. But it won't do you any good if you can't get out again.

Creature From the Depths

Challenge Time: 3 minutes, 15 seconds

Send it back — in a hurry!

Mysterious Orbit

Challenge Time: 6 minutes

Don't let it send you into orbit.

The All-Seeing Eyes

Challenge Time: 8 minutes

Stay cool. You don't need three eyes to beat this beast.

Solutions

pp. 4-5   Night Riders

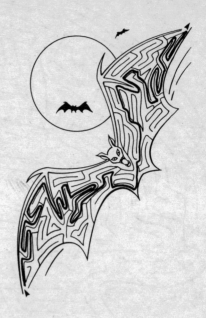

pp. 6-7   Creepy Cat's Cradle

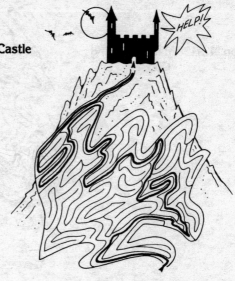

pp. 12-13 **The Trembling Ghost**

pp. 14-15 **Venomous Vampire**

pp. 16-17   The Coffin Caper

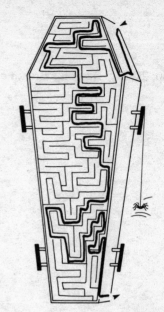

pp. 18-19   The Witching Hour

pp. 20-21   Dragon's Breath

pp. 22-23   Numb Skull

pp. 24-25 Witches Stew

pp. 26-27 Electronic Maniac

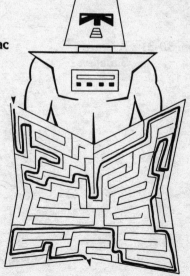

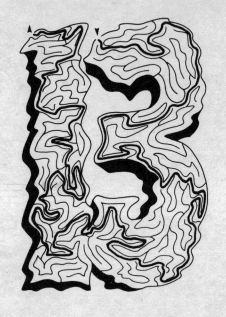

pp. 32-33   The Spider Trap

pp. 34-35   The Claw!

pp. 40-41 **Weirdwolf**

pp. 42-43 **U.F.O. Oh, Oh!**

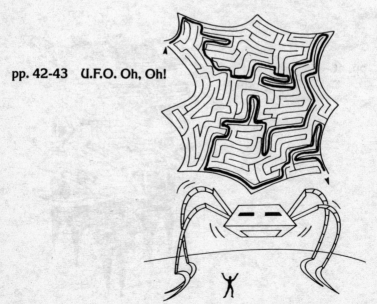

pp. 44-45   Curse of the Great Pyramid

pp. 46-47   Creature From the Depths

pp. 48-49   Mysterious Orbit

pp. 50-51   The All-Seeing Eyes

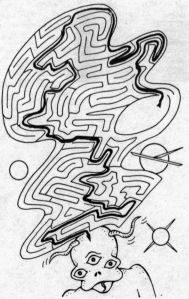